LEADERS OF
ANCIENT GREECE

PERICLES   The Rise and
Fall of Athenian
Democracy

LEADERS OF ANCIENT GREECE

PERICLES

The Rise and Fall of Athenian Democracy

Hamish Aird

Published in 2004 by The Rosen Publishing Group, Inc.
29 East 21st Street, New York, NY 10010

Library of Congress Cataloging-in-Publication Data

Aird, Hamish.
Pericles: the rise and fall of Athenian democracy / by
Hamish Aird.
    p. cm. — (Leaders of ancient Greece)
Includes bibliographical references and index.
ISBN 0-8239-3828-X
1. Pericles, 499–429 B.C. 2. Athens (Greece)—Politics and
government. 3. Democracy—Greece—Athens—History—To
1500. 4. Statesmen—Greece—Athens—Biography.
5. Orators—Greece—Athens—Biography. I. Title. II. Series.
DF228.P4 A37 2003
938'.5—dc21

                                        2002009627

Manufactured in the United States of America

Contents

GREECE AT THE TIME OF PERICLES

BLACK SEA

MACEDONIA   THRACE

• Sigeum

• Acanthus

AEGEAN SEA

• Phocaea

• Ephesus

• Chalcis

Delphi •   Thebes •   • Eritrea

• Miletus

• Athens

PELOPONNESE   • Corinth

Olympia •   Argos •   • Halicarnassus

• Sparta

IONIAN SEA

CRETE

MEDITERRANEAN SEA

INTRODUCTION

The year is 431 BC, and we are standing at the top of a gentle slope looking across to the rocky volcanic outcrop called the Acropolis, the oldest and most sacred part of the city of Athens. The buildings on the Acropolis have only recently been completed. There is the Parthenon, the temple of the city's patron goddess, Athena, and the great monumental gateway known as the Propylaea. As we glance down past the Acropolis we see the bustling city center, or agora, where people are crowded together in groups, buying, selling, arguing, and discussing. The buildings surrounding the agora are less imposing than the Parthenon up on the hill, but even from this distance they are distinctive and suggest a society full of confidence. Beyond the city center are private houses crowded together, cramped within the city walls. The city is surrounded by strong fortifications, and through one of the main gates there is a stream of traffic, horsemen, carriages, carts, and people on foot, heading for the long straight road, flanked by its fortified walls, which leads to Athens's port, Piraeus.

We can see the blue sea some five miles away to the east glinting in the sun, and Athens's great port, walled itself, seems totally secure. Even at this distance we can make out the sleek warships maneuvering in the coastal waters, their many oars catching the sunlight in a perfect rhythm. Clear, too, is the island of Salamis, where the mighty Persian emperor and his fleet were totally defeated some fifty years previously. Dim in the distance to the south is the outline of the hills of the Peloponnese, where lie Corinth and Sparta, the Greek cities most hostile to Athens.

If we turn away from the sea we notice the hills that protect Athens—the gentle slopes of Hymettus, famous for its honey; Mount Pentelikon, with jagged scars where the marble has been quarried for Athens's fine buildings; and to the north Mount Parnes, where a series of garrison forts protect the city's northern approaches. All seems bustling, open, and confident. Athens,

An artist's reconstruction of the Acropolis, the high hill at the center of Athens upon which the Temple of Athena, patron goddess of the city, and the Parthenon could be found.

The ruins of the Acropolis today

after several years of uneasy peace, is now at war with her neighbors in the Peloponnese. The sense of confidence, however, is still evident.

Every Athenian citizen remembers the great wars of 490 BC and 480 to 479 BC, when this tiny city took on the powerful Persian Empire, whose boundaries stretched from the coast of Turkey in the west to the Himalayas in the east, from Russia in the north to Egypt and

Africa in the south. Now Athens is secure against the tyranny from the east, for just seventeen years before those wars Athens had adopted a new system of government, a system known as democracy, or the rule of the people.

Almost all city-states in Greece up to this time had been ruled by either kings, tyrants who gained their power with armed support, or oligarchies, where power was held by a small group of rich nobles or landowners. Each city-state was fiercely proud of its independence. The idea of being part of a country would have had little meaning for an ancient Greek. You were part of your city. There is nothing quite like it today, though perhaps a modern citizen of New York City or Singapore or Berlin might know something of that feeling of pride and independence. When the Persian threat materialized, it took a huge effort, mainly by Athens, the only democratic state, to draw together the Greek cities to act in unison.

The ruins of the Temple of Athena on the Acropolis

By 479 BC the wars were over. Though they got as far as burning Athens and destroying all its old buildings and temples, the Persians were totally defeated. Athens had played a central role in the defeat of the Persians and had emerged as a powerful state with over 200 warships manned mainly by her own oarsmen, the same citizens who had the power to vote for peace or war in the city assembly.

And so with the Persians retreating toward home, the Athenians took over the leadership of the other Greek city-states to ensure that Greece would never again be in danger of such a threat. An independent League of States was formed "to promote the war against the Persians and to make the Aegean Sea safe." At first this league seemed to be a group of equal states voluntarily uniting with a common purpose. Soon, however, the Athenians came to dominate the alliance, refusing to allow some cities to withdraw from the league and forcing other cities to join. In due course, instead of contributing ships and men to the alliance, many states found it easier to contribute money to Athens and to let her do the policing. Having dismissed their own oarsmen, these cities were now no longer able to defend themselves. They depended on Athens.

Another view of the ruins of the Acropolis, photographed from the site of the agora, the ancient marketplace

And so the Athenian Empire was born. It was not an empire as we usually understand the word, gained by conquest and brilliant campaigns by a great general and leader like Alexander or Tamburlaine or Caesar. It was an empire achieved gradually, as the Athenians let their Greek allies know that they were now Athens's subjects.

This was the world in which Pericles grew up. He was born around 495 BC, only about twelve years after democracy came to Athens. His family was aristocratic and rich. His father had been an important figure in the early days of the democracy and had come from a noble family where all the male members would be expected to take a part in the political life of the city. Five years old at the time of the Battle of Marathon, in his teens during the campaign against the second Persian invasion, and in his twenties during the growth of Athenian power, he came to see democracy as essential to Athens at a time when other aristocratic families would have preferred to control the government themselves. But he also saw that if democracy was to work, it needed to be guided by a firm hand. By 430 BC he had come to dominate the Assembly of the Athenian people, which made all the important decisions for the state. The historian Thucydides described him in this way:

> During the whole period of peacetime when Pericles was at the head of affairs the state was wisely led and firmly guarded, and it was under him that Athens was at her greatest.

THE YOUNG PERICLES

We can picture Pericles growing up in one of those plain white houses within the walls of Athens. All around there would have been a lot of building activity, first of the fortifications and then of the houses. The Persians had been very systematic in their destruction of the city in 480 BC. Famous leaders and politicians visited Pericles' home all the time, and the young boy would have breathed in the excitement of the discussions about Persia and the new democratic Athens. We have few descriptions of his physical appearance, though the historian Plutarch tells us of Pericles that "physically he was almost perfect, the only exception being his head, which was rather long and out of proportion." An intelligent and serious boy, he must have picked up information quickly, and he must have been well aware that one day he would be expected, like his father, to play his part in the public life of Athens.

His father, Xanthippus, had been an influential figure in Athens in the 490s and 480s BC when Athens was facing the threat of a Persian invasion. Indeed, Xanthippus had been in command of the forces that had defeated the Persians at Mycale off the coast of Ionia in 479 BC, the same day that the Persians had been defeated in Greece itself at the Battle of Plataea. Pericles' mother, Agariste, was around the house almost all the time, and from her he would have picked up many ideas and an awareness of his family's importance. She came from one of the most influential families in Athens. It was actually her uncle, Cleisthenes, who had introduced democracy to Athens in 507 BC.

As a little boy Pericles also saw much of his *paidagogos*, a family slave whose main job was to look after him and see that he came to no harm. In Athens at this time there were more slaves than free Athenians. Certainly the Athenians of the time never thought there was anything wrong in one person owning another person, and valued household slaves had close links to their

A marble bust of the Athenian leader Pericles

families. The paidagogos explained to Pericles the importance of good behavior and respect for his elders. But there was time for fun, too. One day they played board games together, the next they were out discovering the nature of this great city.

Pericles was a spirited boy, and soon more formal teaching was needed for him. Indeed it is said that when his mother was about to give birth a prophecy was made that she would give birth to a lion cub! By the time he was entering his teens, it would have become clear to his parents that this intelligent, inquisitive, strong-willed boy needed rather special teachers.

A boy from Pericles' background was usually educated in three areas. One teacher taught him reading and writing, and he would have learned many passages from the poet Homer, who had written famous stories of the Trojan Wars. Most Athenians were literate, and Pericles learned to read and to write on wax tablets. Another teacher introduced the young boy to music, for the Athenians regarded music as an essential part of schooling. They believed that music had a moral effect on pupils. Good music produced upright, loyal citizens. Bad music, on the other hand, had a corrupting influence. Pericles might have learned to play the flute and the lyre, a stringed instrument somewhat like a modern guitar. A third teacher taught him athletics: running, jumping, throwing the javelin and discus, wrestling, and even boxing. This would take place in the *palaestra*, a square training area with colonnades all round where the boys could rest in the shade. Athletes exercised naked and before starting would coat their bodies with olive oil. After exercise they scraped the oil and grime off and took cold baths. Athletics were important for two reasons. Many of the state festivals had athletic contests, and a young person from a good family would be expected to compete in them. Furthermore, Athens was a military state, and from an early age Pericles knew the importance of being physically fit and able, if necessary, to fight for his city. Ancient writers do not tell us

This vase painting depicts a sacrificial bull being led to the altar. Note the musicians, who were an essential part of the ritual.

specifically whether Pericles had this sort of education, but it is very likely that he did. What they do tell us is that his parents, aware that they had a very special son, engaged two very special teachers for him, Damon and Anaxagoras.

Damon was Pericles' music teacher, and he had a very strong influence on his pupil. All teachers were expected not just to teach subjects but also to develop qualities of good behavior and character in their pupils. Damon continued to develop Pericles' knowledge of Homer and also taught him how to sing and play the lyre. He would also want to prepare his young pupil for public life. Damon made Pericles aware of the responsibilities that lay ahead of him as a member of one of the foremost families in Athens. For Damon, as well as being a teacher of music, was also interested in philosophy and politics, and he saw his job as preparing Pericles for the contests of political life.

Pericles' other teacher was Anaxagoras, a much more famous Greek than Damon. Anaxagoras came from Clazomenae, one of the Greek towns on the coast of Ionia, in modern Turkey, where men had recently started to ask questions about the great issues of life. Where do we come from? What is the world made of? What is the nature of the stars and the sun and

When an animal was sacrificially slaughtered, a portion of the meat was dedicated to the gods and burned on the altar.

the moon? How ought men to behave toward each other? What can we learn from mathematics? It was Anaxagoras who encouraged Pericles to ask questions, to search for the natural causes of events, rather than putting everything down to the gods. A story is told how once Pericles was sent a ram's head that had just one central horn, like a unicorn. A soothsayer, who was employed to find religious meanings for strange things like this, said that this meant that Pericles would soon be the one important politician in the city. But Anaxagoras took the ram's head, opened it up, and showed that it was a deformation of the skull that had led to the single horn, nothing to do with the gods but arising from a natural cause. In modern terms, Anaxagoras taught Pericles to use his common sense.

Anaxagoras also taught Pericles a skill that was destined to set him apart from all his contemporaries: how to speak in public. In ancient Greece there were few books, as they were very expensive and difficult to keep in the form of clay tablets. Therefore, speaking person to person was the normal method of communication. The Athenians loved talking and were famous for it. The spoken word was important in many different areas: in politics, when the people met to make decisions on important matters; in the theater, where the audience had to be moved by the playwright's words; in the lawcourts; and even at dinner parties, where an Athenian of Pericles' background was expected to talk convincingly about a wide variety of topics. The skills that Pericles showed in his mastery of the art of speaking were greatly admired, and it was Anaxagoras who had shown him the way.

Many of the best teachers of debating and public speaking in the Greek world were attracted to Athens and were known as Sophists. They charged fees and would gather groups of pupils round them. Some would teach more theoretical subjects like astronomy or mathematics, while others taught their pupils how to get on in the world of politics or law. The vitality of Athens and the openness of the Athenians to new ideas encouraged these Sophists to come to Athens and often to stay for many years.

Yet perhaps even more important than formal schooling was the atmosphere in Athens during these exciting days. Only five years old at the time, Pericles was probably unaware of the great Battle of Marathon, where the Persian expeditionary force was defeated and turned back. But ten years later, he would have felt the apprehension in the city as the Persians made preparations in 490 BC for another mammoth expedition to punish Athens once and for all. Pericles' contemporary, the historian Herodotus, tells us that the Persian army numbered five million men. Even allowing for considerable exaggeration, it must have been a mighty expedition. The Greek allies defeated this army and navy in three important battles when Pericles was about fifteen or sixteen years old. It would have captured his imagination, and it is not hard to imagine him rushing down to greet his father as he sailed back victoriously into the port of Piraeus with his fleet of triremes, or warships.

This is a vase painting of Dionysus, the god of wine and ecstasy. The Athenians celebrated two festivals dedicated to Dionysus every year.

A boy of such spirit must have been itching to fight himself, not least because, with other Athenians, he had suffered the shame of being forced to leave his home in the city and seek refuge on the island of Salamis as the Persian army drew near.

From his teachers Damon and Anaxagoras, and from all the talk at home, Pericles came to realize how these victories had been the result of the bravery and spirit of the ordinary Athenians who fought in the ranks and rowed in the fleet. He would have known that they were fighting not for a king or a tyrant or a few nobles, but for themselves and their own government. Every Athenian citizen had a say in all important decisions.

THE YOUNG POLITICIAN

In 477 BC, Pericles had just come of age. He was eighteen years old and could now take a full part in Athenian life. For someone of his background, this meant, above all, a political life, but first he would have had a year of military service with the Athenian army. This might have involved guarding one of the forts that protected Athens to the north. Or he may have been involved in one of the campaigns against the Persians in the 470s BC, when Athens led the other Greek states in a drive to make all the seas around Greece safe from Persian harassment. In later years, Pericles was a renowned general, so it is likely he had plenty of war experience as a young man. He would have become acquainted with Cimon, the great commander responsible for laying the foundations of the Athenian Empire.

A bronze statue of a Greek warrior, possibly by the sculptor Pheidias

Cimon had served under Pericles' father in the Persian Wars. But campaigning usually only happened in the warm summer months. Therefore, young Pericles was home at Athens most of the year.

Here for the very first time he became actively involved in political life. In those early years, he was very much just an observer, watching, studying how democracy worked, biding his time, learning the skills of a politician, and making influential friends. Once a week or so, he walked to the Pnyx, where the Assembly of all adult male Athenians met in the open air. Each time he passed the Acropolis, the striking outcrop of rock that dominates the city, he remembered the temples that used to adorn it and the new temple to Athena still being built when the Persians attacked. Now, as he made his way up to the Pnyx, all he could see were broken and burnt stones and charred wood, a scene of complete desolation. The Athenians had vowed that until they had eliminated the Persian threat forever, the Acropolis would remain as a bleak memorial of the terrible days when the enemy had entered and sacked their city in 480 BC. One day, he must have said to himself, I will rebuild those temples!

At the Pnyx in the open air he would have joined several thousand other Athenians to discuss state business and to make decisions. In the streets near the Pnyx were policemen, called Scythian archers, who carried whips dipped in red dye, ready to mark any citizens trying to avoid going to the Assembly. Those marked in this way would be liable for a fine, for it was regarded as a citizen's duty to attend the Assembly. First the members of the Council arrived. There were 500 of them, and their job was to prepare business for the Assembly and to enforce the Assembly's decisions. They were all over thirty years of age and came from all over Athens and Attica. They met each day in the Council House half a mile from the Pnyx. They represented a cross section of Athenian society, and they were picked by lot in their villages and neighborhoods. The Athenians favored selection by lot. It ensured that a variety of citizens from different classes and back-grounds were in public positions, and it made bribery very difficult!

Perhaps the issue would be the construc-tion of a new road down to the silver mines south of Athens. The Council would have already discussed this and would have pro-duced motions in support of the measure for the ordinary citizens of the Assembly to vote on. Before the Assembly's vote, any Athenian had the right to speak for or against the motion. We know that Pericles tended only to speak on matters that he thought particularly important, so he might not have weighed in on every issue. Also present at the debate were the ten generals, each one of them elected for a year. Their job was to lead the army and the navy, but they were also respected by the people for their opinions on non-military matters. In peacetime, though they had no power to overturn the verdict of the people, they could exert considerable political influence. Pericles would have noticed how even these important

These bronze voting disks were used by the Athenians to decide verdicts in court cases.

Athenians had to persuade the citizens if they wanted anything done. Soon a vote was taken by a show of hands.

This form of direct democracy, where every citizen has his say, is very different from modern democracies, where ordinary citizens are only asked to vote every two or four years, and where laws are approved by elected representatives rather than everyone. Modern states are too big for direct democracy to work, but the Athenian democracy provided the blueprint for all later democracies. Of course, even the Athenian democracy had its failings. No women were allowed into the Assembly. They had no

A vase painting of a young man learning to play the lyre, a string instrument

political say at all. Slaves were not allowed to take part, and there were more slaves living in Athens and Attica than freeborn citizens. Nor were foreigners residing in Athens allowed the vote, however long they had lived in the city.

The Athenians had another method of checking the ambitions of powerful individuals. They used a system called ostracism. A meeting of the Assembly would decide whether an ostracism should be held, and then all the citizens would write the name of the person that they wanted to leave the city on a small piece of pottery called an ostracon. The pieces of pottery were then counted and the person whose name appeared most often was expelled from the city for ten years. Many of these ostracons have been found by archaeologists in the agora in Athens, including some with the name of Pericles' father and Pericles himself.

It is hard not to admire the Athenian system, especially with hindsight, when we see what the Athenians achieved in the short space of time when they held their empire. Pericles as a young man in his twenties went regularly to the Assembly and saw how important the ordinary Athenian citizen was. Even though he was of noble birth himself, Pericles understood that any future development of Athens must have as its foundation these ordinary Athenians. Above all, these same citizens were the men who manned the Athenian fleet, and the fleet would be at the heart of Athens's success.

Throughout the 470s and the 460s BC, Athens and her allies were still at war against the Persians, both to extract money from them for the cost of the earlier campaigns and to make the Aegean Sea safe for Greek trading. Much of the success of Athens in these campaigns was due to Cimon, an inspired and popular general. Various expeditions that he led had culminated in a mighty victory for the Athenians in 467 BC at Eurymedon in southern Turkey, where the entire fleet of 200 Persian ships was destroyed. We do not know if Pericles was with the Athenian forces for this battle, but we do know that from this time on the Persians were no longer a serious threat and the Greek cities could start to think in terms of a peaceful future.

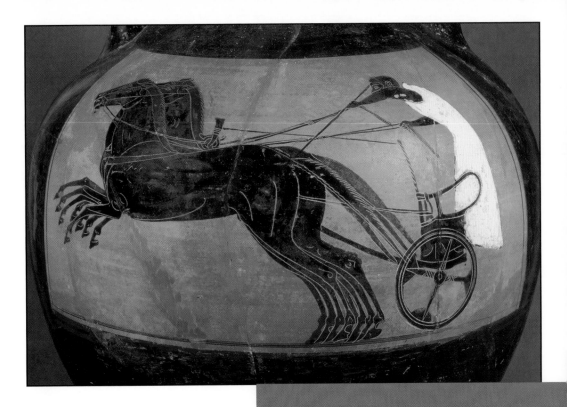

This vase depicts a charioteer racing his team of horses.

Many of the allies who had helped Athens in these campaigns now wanted to disband the army and navy and go home. Cimon and the other Athenians, however, were unhappy about this, and a number of city-states were now forced by Athens to stay in the alliance. One such state was Thasos, a powerful city in the north Aegean that in 465 BC revolted against the Athenian alliance. Cimon set about besieging the city, but he knew that such a siege would keep him away from Athens for years.

Pericles was now in his thirties and ready to make his mark on the political scene. He had

formed an alliance with an Athenian called Ephialtes, who shared his views about democracy and the importance of including ordinary Athenians in the government of the state. Their natural opponents were Cimon and his supporters, who wanted to keep the more traditional form of government in which an assembly of older and richer Athenians, called the Areopagus, made the important decisions. Together Pericles and Ephialtes set about reducing the powers of the Areopagus and transferring them to the Assembly and the Council. There was some opposition to this from members of the upper classes, some of whom had been prosecuted in the courts by Pericles and Ephialtes, and Ephialtes was killed in street fighting. Suddenly Pericles found himself the man of the hour,

A vase painting of a musician playing an aulos, a wind instrument

and, angry at the death of his friend, he led the Assembly to pass the reform measures that would guarantee the power of the ordinary people in Athens. In the excitement of the moment, the people forgot about the great successes of Cimon and his development of their empire, and they ostracized him and turned to Pericles as their main leader.

For the next thirty years, Pericles, by his unique ability for public speaking, was to dominate the Assembly at Athens and develop the democracy. Plutarch tells us about Pericles' noble qualities, his incorruptibility, his honesty, and his refusal to make himself popular. What we see in Athens in 461 BC, however, is a great surge of energy and a willingness to take on a whole range of military commitments all over the Mediterranean. Under Cimon, the Athenian Empire developed steadily and sensibly. Under Pericles, there was a period of huge activity and bold initiatives before he came to see the sensible and wise way forward.

WAR

From an early age, Pericles knew that he would be expected to fight for his country and that the prospect of death in battle was a very real one. Indeed, throughout his life from 495 BC to 429 BC, apart from one notable period from 446 BC to 431 BC, Athens was almost continually at war. Yet in Athens the atmosphere was not warlike and there was no feeling of being in a military state. Athenians went about their daily business, perhaps as craftsmen, shopkeepers, farmers, or traders, and only when a campaign was to be fought did they take up arms, ready to march or sail to wherever they were commanded. They knew that the price of keeping an empire was to be ready to defend it. And normally a campaign would only last for a few months in the summer.

The Athenian army was made up almost entirely of its well-to-do citizens. As a hoplite, or infantryman, you had to be rich enough to afford body armor: a bronze helmet, a breastplate, and leg armor. There was no central government supply of these necessary items. Much of the training for fighting was done during the year of military service that a male citizen had to undergo when he was eighteen, and there is little evidence of regular military combat training beyond this. Indeed, Pericles himself said when addressing the Athenian people:

> We do not have to spend our time practic-
> ing to meet sufferings that are still in the
> future. We meet danger voluntarily with
> an easy mind, instead of with laborious
> training.

This attitude produced a real sense of pride in the Athenian hoplite. He fought in line, and with his shield he protected both himself and the person next to him. Therefore, all those fighting in the line were dependent on each other, and this led to a readiness to risk one's life for the man next to you. Even without regular training, the Athenian hoplites were a force to be reckoned with and won many battles in Pericles' time.

This is a bronze statue of the Charioteer of Delphi, celebrating a victory in a chariot race held at Delphi some time early in the fifth century BC.

The city-state that opposed Athens for much of this period was Sparta. Sparta was a military state in the mountains of the Peloponnese 140 miles (225 kilometers) south of Athens. Here Spartan boys were brought up from their earliest youth to regard war and fighting as the only things that really mattered, and all their education was geared toward military training. Their way of life was simple, and we still describe simple surroundings as being "spartan." All their male citizens were permanently in the army and, while much of their time was spent in keeping the city-states around them under their control, they would also venture out of their home area from time to time to engage in expeditions abroad. They had helped Athens to defeat the Persians in 480 BC. The Athenians might be spirited fighters, but everyone in Greece knew that the Spartan hoplite was supreme. Above all, everyone remembered the famous 300 Spartans who, under their King Leonidas, had fought to the death at the Pass of Thermopylae, holding off the huge army of Xerxes, king of Persia.

One area where Athens had no equal, however, was its navy. In the 480s BC, a far-sighted leader named Themistocles had persuaded the Athenians to use a rich vein of silver that they had found in the mines south of Athens to build a fleet of 200 ships, and this provided the basis for Athenian power. No one was more aware of the importance of this fleet than Pericles himself. There must have been many times that he mounted his horse in the center of Athens and rode down to Piraeus, the great port of Athens some five miles away. He would have galloped out of the Dipylon, or Double Gate, down a long straight road with defensive walls on either side. This road linked Athens to its naval base. At Piraeus there were three naval

This vase painting is of an owl sitting on a branch.

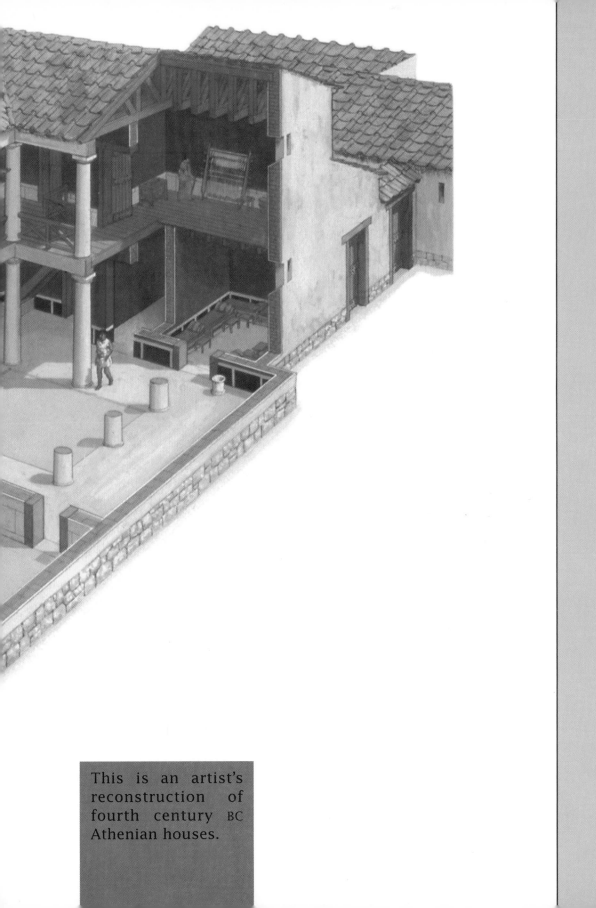

This is an artist's reconstruction of fourth century BC Athenian houses.

harbors and a thriving commercial port. Two of the naval harbors were shaped like horseshoes and surrounded by sheds where the Athenian warships were docked. Each ship had its individual shed and the foundations of some of these can still be seen today. All around were warehouses storing equipment for the ships, such as masts, sails, oars, and ropes.

The Athenian warship was called a trireme. It had three banks of oars manned by 170 oarsmen. Above the rowing levels there was a flat deck where up to twenty marines stood ready to board enemy ships if necessary, or to repel boarders. About 100 feet (30 meters) long and only 9 feet (3 meters) wide, the trireme was basically a floating guided missile. At the bow was a bronze ram head, and the aim in fighting was to drive this into the side of an enemy ship and sink it. Recently a reconstruction of a trireme has been built in Athens. The sea trials conducted have proved what a lethal weapon it was.

It is often thought that these ships were rowed by slaves, as was the case with oared galleys from Roman times onward. This was not so. The Athenian triremes were rowed by freemen, either Athenian citizens or their allies. The citizens were those same people who supported Pericles in the Assembly and who Pericles knew were essential to Athens's success. In cramped conditions and with great discomfort, unable to see anything but the back of the rower in front of him, the Athenian oarsman knew two things: he was the best oarsman in the world and he was his own master.

It must have been an amazing sight when those 200 ships, manned by 34,000 oarsmen, were at sea, each with their 170 oars all moving in perfect rhythm. Foreign visitors to the city would have been in no doubt about the nature of Athens's power and supremacy. The historian Thucydides describes a huge expedition—at least 100 warships with many transport ships, too—that sailed for Sicily some time after Pericles' death:

> When the ships were manned and everything had been taken aboard, silence was commanded by the sound of a trumpet, and the customary prayers made before putting to sea were offered up, not by each ship separately but by them all together following the words of a herald. The crowds on the shore also, the citizens and others who wished well to the expedition, joined together in the prayers. Then

when the hymn had been sung, they put out to sea, first sailing out in column, and then racing each other as far as the island of Aegina.

These then were the forces that were available to Athens in the middle of the fifth century BC—forces bolstered and guided by the political scene in Athens.

It must have been with some surprise that Pericles found himself the main political leader in Athens in 461 BC. He might have expected to have Ephialtes sharing the responsibility with him, but Ephialtes had been assassinated and there was unlikely to be any strong opposition to his leadership, as Cimon had just been ostracized for ten years. Pericles was relatively free to pursue the policies he wanted. He not only wanted to increase the size of Athens's empire abroad, he also wanted to extend Athens's power nearer to home.

A number of military actions over the next ten years make it clear that he hoped to develop a land empire that would include Megara, a town some thirty miles from Athens on the Isthmus of Corinth, and also the state of Boeotia to the north of Athens. He never lost sight of the importance of Athens's naval power, however. At the heart of

A modern artist's rendering of the typical clothing worn by ancient Greek men and women

his policy was the idea that Athens and her port should be as formidable and closely linked as possible. With this in mind, he set about building a third long wall to connect Athens with Piraeus even more securely.

At the same time, in 460 BC, Pericles sent off a large expedition of 200 ships to Cyprus and Egypt. Egypt had been part of the Persian Empire for a long time. At first the expedition was successful, but soon it was unable to make any further progress up the Nile River. At home, Athens came into conflict with a number of her neighbors when she decided to form an alliance with Megara. The two states most upset by this were Corinth, also situated on the isthmus, 30 miles (48 kilometers) from Megara, and Sparta. Over the next fifteen years, there were a number of clashes between Athens and these two states. Pericles was never slow to send forces out to look after Athens's interests.

Pericles also decided to permanently subdue the island of Aegina, which was an old enemy, visible from the coast of Athens. Indeed, Pericles had referred to it sometime earlier as "the eye-sore of Piraeus." Even the disastrous end to the Egyptian expedition in 454 BC, with virtually no survivors returning to Athens, did not deter the Athenians. They continued to fight with their neighbors to the north in Boeotia and to the south in the Peloponnese. At sea, the Athenians were almost always victorious. When they fought on land, they often came off worse.

At times, the Athenian forces were massively overstretched, so much so that on one occasion they had to dispatch a force composed entirely of old men and boys under the age of eighteen to fight and win against the Corinthians in 459 BC. This engagement was destined to have important consequences, for it ended with the Athenians penning up the Corinthian forces in a small enclosure and pelting them all to death. The Corinthians would never forget the shame and the brutality of this act. Finally, in 446 BC, Athens's most important ally, the island of Euboea, some fifty miles north of Athens, revolted from the alliance and declared her independence. Pericles himself went out with a force of hoplites, suppressed the revolt, and forced the people of Euboea to stay in the empire.

The years 461 BC to 446 BC were difficult for Athens, and it is not always easy to see why Pericles was prepared to take so many risks and fight on so many different fronts. There were moments when the Spartans and their allies could have broken Athens's power if they had been prepared to take the initiative. It was a close-run rivalry from this point on. While ensuring that the empire held together, Pericles developed a more cautious policy toward Corinth and Sparta and their allies. Peace was made with Corinth and Sparta in 446 BC, and this complemented a peace that had been made three years earlier with the Persians. Suddenly, after years of fighting, both against Persia and her Greek neighbors, Athens was finally no longer at war. Pericles was coming up on his fiftieth birthday, and he had an important job to do.

THE GOLDEN YEARS

Pericles had achieved much in the years up to 446 BC, but he now embarked on the program that was to ensure that his name and the name of Athens would never be forgotten. Now was the time to ensure that in peace Athens would achieve even more than she had in war.

Athens in 446 BC was a city unlike any other. Crowds from all over the known world mingled in the streets of the city and its port, Piraeus. The Athenian people themselves felt a new confidence after their wars with the Persians and the other Greek city-states, but they were not overconfident. There had been losses in battle, and many families had lost sons in the fighting. With peace gained, the multitude of oarsmen who manned the fleet were no longer required to serve the warships full-time, and they were looking for other work.

Work began on the Parthenon in 447 BC and was finished in 432 BC. Its construction was symbolic of Athenian imperial power and the influence of Pericles.

New buildings had sprung up in the narrow confines of the city walls—public buildings, shops, and shrines to the gods. In Piraeus, a corn exchange and a market had been constructed, and the town around the port itself had been built up

with planned streets running at right angles, wide and easy for transport. But one place still stood desolate and in ruins nearly fifty years after it had been burned by the Persians—the Acropolis.

Now was the time to rebuild these temples and to make the Acropolis a marvel for all time. Pericles had been thinking about this all his adult life. Almost every day since he had become a leader, Pericles must have been waiting for the right moment. He would need a good architect, the best in the world, and he would need many skilled craftsmen from all over the Greek world, and even more laborers. He would need money and he would need peace to enable the works to go ahead without interruption. At hand he had the services of those citizens who had been under his command in the fleet and were now looking for new employment.

In an attempt to bring the Greek cities together, Pericles had proposed a motion in the Assembly two years earlier in 448 BC, a year after peace was made with Persia. This motion invited all the Greek cities to send delegates to a grand meeting at Athens. The matters to be discussed were the Greek temples that had been burned down, not just in Athens but all over the Greek world, as well as the whole question of the security of the seas. Even though invitations were sent out, the Spartans were already beginning to fear the growth of Athenian power, and under their influence all the other states refused the invitation. Perhaps they all knew that what was really at stake was not just new buildings for Athens, but also a tacit acknowledgment of Athens's leading status. Athens would have to go it alone.

The first task was to build a new temple to Athena, the patron goddess of the city. For forty-five years, she had been without a proper home, and this temple had to outshine all other temples in Greece. To ensure that all went smoothly, a director of buildings was appointed. He was the sculptor Pheidias, who was a friend of Pericles'. The architects for the great new temple were to be Callicrates and Ictinus.

Individual architects were appointed for other buildings. There must have been many discussions before the first stone was laid. But the deciding factor in any argument was always that it must be the very best possible.

And so the Parthenon of Athena began to rise from the volcanic rock of the Acropolis. People were amazed to see the shining white marble blocks of stone as they were pulled along specially made roads from Mount Pentelicon by teams of oxen. Temples in those days were normally built of limestone or sandstone. Marble was far more difficult to work with and cost almost ten times more than ordinary stone. Slowly the partly carved blocks were hauled up onto the Acropolis, where skilled craftsmen and sculptors waited to work on them. We have accounts from this period listing the wages paid to workmen and showing how free citizens, foreign workers, and slaves worked side by side. Many of those workers would be the oarsmen, who with peace were no longer required to row all the time. They had fought to build the Athenian Empire. Now they were competing to make the most beautiful temple in the world.

The task facing Callicrates and Ictinus was not an easy one. In line with tradition, the

temple was rectangular with a row of circular columns on all four sides supporting the roof. There also had to be a large interior room that would act as the home for a huge statue of Athena, and another room to hold the treasures of the goddess. There had to be sculptures on the temple to illustrate Athena's life and her relationship with the Athenian people. The temple had to be large enough to be truly impressive in its own right. It had to have the most secure of foundations and be visible from miles away.

All these problems were overcome, and within five years the Parthenon stood on the Acropolis, marking the power of the city and the devotion of the Athenians to their goddess. It was 210 feet (70 meters) long by 100 feet (31 meters) wide, and the entrance faced east. From the outside the marble would have shined brilliantly in the sun, but if you looked up you would have seen painted carvings decorating the temple. Most impressive would have been those in the pediments, or triangular areas at the top of the columns at each end. One showed the birth of Athena. She was supposed in Athenian myth to have sprung fully armed from the head of Zeus, her father. At the other end in the pediment was a depiction of the contest between Athena and the sea god Poseidon to decide who should control Athens and Attica. The story goes that Athena offered the people the olive tree and so won their loyalty.

Two other features have caught the imagination of people ever since. As you went up the steps into the temple, above your head inside the columns there was a continuous carving 600 feet (200 meters) long that showed a stately procession to Athena, honoring the day each year when a new robe was offered by the people to their goddess. This frieze, as elevated wall carvings are called, still exists and is in the British Museum in London, England. Copies of it exist all round the world, and it is famous for the nobility and realism of its carvings. Even more impressive than this was the huge statue of Athena, 30 feet (10 meters) high, seated on her throne inside the dimly lit temple and shining with gold and ivory. Pheidias himself made this statue and constructed it with plates of gold. The statue was pillaged many centuries ago and now we have only small copies of it that date from Roman times.

There is no doubt that Pericles saw the worship of Athena as central to the future of Athens. Each year she had her own festival that started with a procession from the Kerameikos,

This detail from the frieze on the upper edge of the Parthenon no longer, of course, shows its painted colors.

or funeral area of Athens at the Dipylon Gate. The procession moved through the agora past all the most important official buildings in Athens, and then wound its way up to the Acropolis. It is no surprise that Pheidias chose to portray this procession so wonderfully in the Parthenon frieze. It contained horsemen, hoplites, officials, and flute players, and animals being led to sacrifice. The festival itself included an exciting night race with runners carrying torches, followed the next day by competitions and contests and more sacrifices. Over a hundred animals were sacrificed, and every four years, when the great festival to Athena was celebrated, the contests and sacrifices were even more elaborate.

So impressive was the Parthenon that no later conqueror of Athens ever thought of destroying it. The Parthenon, however, was just part of a much bigger building program. This

included a grand ceremonial entrance to the Acropolis called the Propylaea, which would also act as a picture gallery for the best of Athenian paintings. It was built after the Parthenon had been completed and is perhaps the greatest of all ceremonial gateways. An incident, which Plutarch relates, tells of the close interest that Pericles took in the actual building. A craftsman working at a great height slipped and fell to the ground. He lay there severely injured and the doctors told

Pericles that the man was unlikely to recover. The goddess Athena then appeared to Pericles in a dream and suggested a course of treatment. He saw that the course of treatment was given to the man, who quickly recovered. In due course Pericles had a statue of Athena the Healer set up on the Acropolis to commemorate the event.

All over Attica splendid temples and public buildings were rising. Pericles wanted everyone in Attica to feel part of this Athenian renaissance. Some of these buildings were in small villages, some on the borders with Boeotia, some by the sea. The most famous is the Temple of Poseidon at Sunium on the southernmost tip of Attica. Poseidon was the god of the sea and second in importance only to Athena for the Athenians. The remains of his gleaming white marble temple stand high above the sea and can still be seen by sailors as a notable landmark from miles away. Below the temple, hewn out of the rock of the cliff face, was a boat shed for two fast rowing boats that could be launched at a moment's notice to bring news of any dangers to the city. Pericles was always aware that Athens must protect her territories and protect these beautiful new buildings.

The ruins of the Temple of Poseidon overlook the sea at Sunium.

Not surprisingly, some people were envious of Pericles' achievements, and up until 443 BC he was attacked in the Assembly because of the apparent extravagance of the building program. After 443 BC there was little criticism of

Pericles himself, but his opponents had no hesitation about attacking his friends. Rumors flew round about Pheidias. People claimed that he had cheated the state when making the gold and ivory statue of Athena for the Parthenon. Plutarch tells us that he died in prison either of sickness or after being poisoned. As long as the buildings still stand, however, Pheidias's reputation will be secure.

It is no coincidence that Athens's greatest playwrights all flourished at the time when Pericles was leading Athens. The greatest of all, Sophocles, was a personal friend of Pericles' throughout their lives. Just as the great buildings are still admired in Athens and Attica, so the plays of Sophocles are still produced all over the world, sometimes in the original Greek, but more often in translation. Their

A front view of the Parthenon today

plots are based on myths or ancient stories handed down from generation to generation. The most famous of these concerns Oedipus, the king of the city of Thebes, and tells how he came to the city as a stranger and saved it from a plague. Hailed as a hero, he marries the queen, a widow, whose husband has been killed by an unknown man some time previously. Oedipus believes that he is the son of the king and queen of the neighboring state, Corinth, but as the story goes on a most horrific truth is revealed. Oedipus's real father was the previous king of Thebes, and he himself was the murderer of his father, and he has now married his own mother. Shocked by what he has done, Oedipus blinds himself and is forced to leave the city forever as a wandering beggar.

These plays are known as tragedies, and they usually tell the story of how men or women, as a result of some flaw in their characters or some stroke of bad luck, undergo terrible sufferings handed out by the gods or by fate. It has even been suggested that Sophocles had Pericles in mind when he wrote the story of Oedipus. Certainly in another of his great tragedies, *Antigone*, Sophocles discusses the conflict between the interests of the state and the individual. Antigone's brother has been fighting for the enemy against her own country. He dies and Antigone sees it as her duty to give him a proper burial. But the king of her state, Creon, has ordered that none of the enemy are to be buried. They must be left to rot on the battlefield, and anyone who defies this order will be executed. The strength of Pericles' influence must have been clear to everyone in Athens, and to many, Sophocles' treatment of the story of Antigone would have seemed very relevant.

Certainly drama was immensely important for the Athenians. The theater itself was very different from what we are used to today. Plays were produced only as part of a festival. The Athenians did not have weekends as we do, and instead their year was broken up by a series of sixty or seventy major festival days. Pericles realized the importance of relaxation for the Athenians, and in

his famous funeral speech, delivered in 430 BC, he said:

> When our work is over we are in a position to enjoy all kinds of recreation for our spirits. There are various kinds of contests and sacrifices regularly throughout the year. In our own homes we find a beauty and good taste that delight us every day and drives away our cares.

Originally most of the festivals were connected with the growing of crops and the harvest, but by the fifth century BC, they were more important as times of relaxation for the people. Plays were put on at two great festivals, the Dionysia in March and the Lenaea in December.

Theater buildings had no roofs. In fact, in the earliest times the audience would just sit on a hillside and look down on the performers below. At Athens, the theater was set into the south side of the Acropolis and could hold 17,000 people. Plays would begin soon after dawn and go on for seven hours. In the time of Pericles, the seats were wooden benches. Later, stone was used as the theaters became more permanent. The horseshoe shape of the Greek theater is famous. Many of the theaters were taken over by the Romans and can still be visited today. Right next door to the theater in Athens was the concert hall, or Odeion, that was built by Pericles. It was a covered building with a high roof that was said by comedians to reflect the shape of Pericles' own head. Inside the Odeion, singing and musical contests were held.

Comic masks were used in the ancient Greek theater. Comedy arose out of the Dionysian festivals.

There was considerable excitement on the days of the dramatic festivals. These festivals took the form of competitions between three playwrights with a group of ten ordinary people chosen to act as judges. Just as the Athenian people were very good at listening to arguments in the Assembly, they were skilled at understanding complicated themes and ideas in the plays. Actors wore masks so there were no facial expressions visible, and the words and their delivery were all-important. Women did not

An artist's reconstruction of a Greek theater, where the plays of Sophocles might have been performed

act. All the female roles were played by men.

Apart from the tragedies, comedies were also performed, with fantastic plots, slapstick humor, and comments on topical events in Athens. Aristophanes was the most famous of the comic poets, and he was quite likely to attack leading figures at Athens in his plays. Anything was acceptable in these comedies and there is no doubt that they were very popular with the ordinary people. They had an underlying seriousness, however, and often dealt with themes like the ordinary person's dislike of war. In one well-known passage, Aristophanes attacks Pericles, admittedly after his death, for being too keen to fight with the Spartans. By the late 430s BC, the storm clouds of war were hovering over the city again.

What was domestic life like for Pericles? What was his wife like? For anyone writing today these would be important issues when dealing with an eminent statesman. Ancient writers, however, were not really concerned with these matters. We do not even know the name of Pericles' wife. We know that she had been married before and that she had been the mother of an influential friend of Pericles', Callias. She gave birth to two sons, Xanthippus, named after Pericles' father, and Paralus, but then they separated and she lived with another man. It seems as though the separation was agreed to by both of them, and there is no word of a divorce.

We would probably be most impressed by the simplicity of life in an Athenian household. There was much to do because there were none of the household aids that we take for granted. Much of life was lived outdoors, especially from April through October. Most of the houses that have been uncovered by archaeologists have been simple in design and very different from some of the elaborate Roman villas that have been discovered.

One thing is clear: While women had very little to do with the political and commercial life of Athens, at home they had considerable importance in managing the household. This would include the making of clothes, the provision of food, the cooking, the management of slaves within the household, and the upbringing of the children in the early years. It is clear from Greek literature and from tender scenes on gravestones that relations between husband and wife were often close and affectionate. The fact remains, however, that for women it was a very different life from what we consider acceptable. For example, when there were dinner parties at the better-off homes, wives were not present. The men would have dinner and then discuss politics or philosophy or lighter topics, and they might be entertained by other women, but the wives would remain behind the scenes. In a wealthier home, part of the house was reserved for women and they were expected to keep to this area. There was no formal education for girls, and they would have learned from their mothers only what they needed to know to run a household. Women did have their own special religious festivals where men were not present, but it is unlikely that in Pericles' time they went to the theater, and they certainly did not go to the Assembly.

Yet we know from writers and from scenes on pottery that home life went on, families were brought up, and the family was thought of by most Athenians as being very important. It is still surprising, though, that when Pericles described

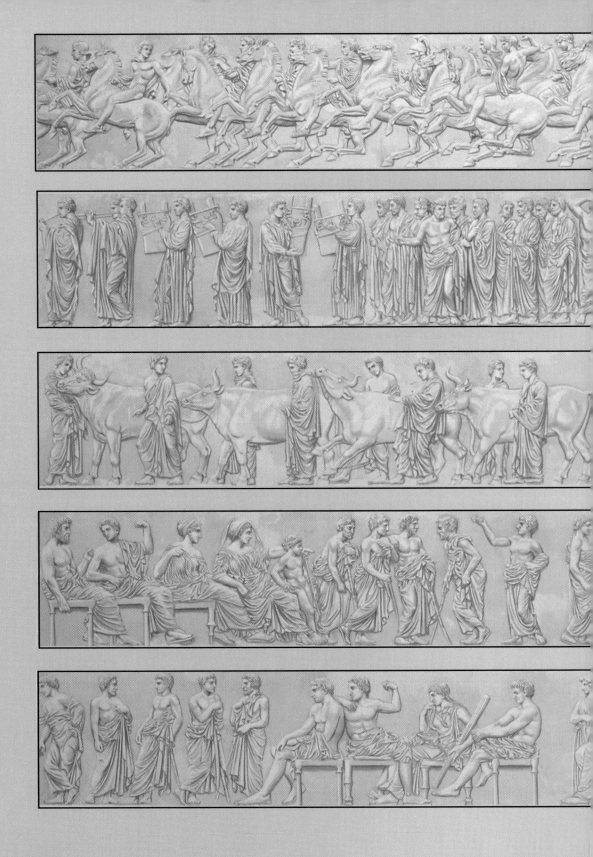

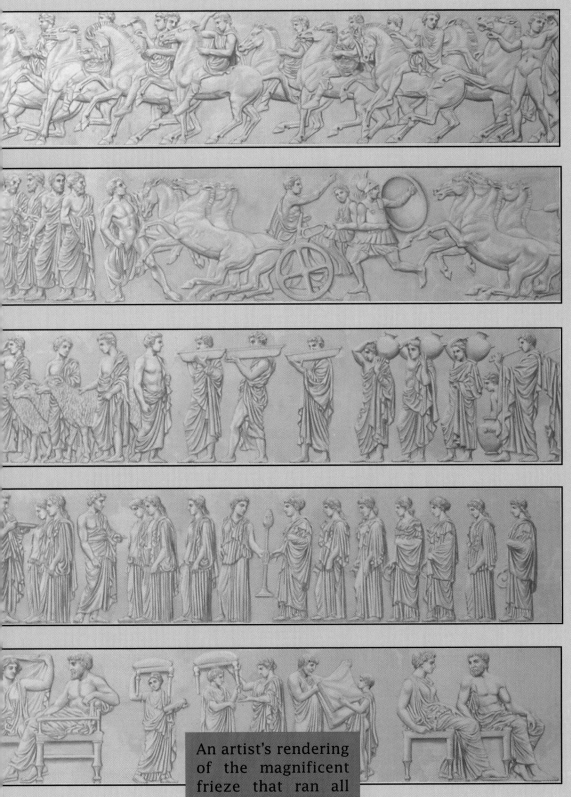

An artist's rendering of the magnificent frieze that ran all around the upper edge of the walls of the Parthenon

the glories of Athens at the end of the first year of war with Sparta, his only words were:

> Your greatest glory is not to be inferior to what God has made you, and the greatest glory of a woman is to be least talked about by men, whether they are praising you or criticizing you.

There was one woman who was very important in Pericles' life apart from his wife. This was Aspasia, who had been born in Miletus in Ionia and who became a close friend and lover of Pericles'. It is likely that she was a highly intelligent person, and Plutarch talks about her "rare political wisdom" and goes on to say how Pericles lived with Aspasia "and loved her dearly." Again, personal enemies of Pericles' tried to get at him by attacking Aspasia. On one occasion when she was prosecuted in the courts for a religious offense, Pericles is said to have burst into tears in the court and begged the jurors to let Aspasia off.

Compared with modern women, an Athenian mother or wife seems to have had a very restricted life, with virtually no education and no real say in how the city was run. This may seem strange to us when we consider that the patron goddess of the city, Athena, was female, and that the plays of the time were full of strong female characters. It is likely that although women were not allowed to play a formal part in the public life of Athens, they nonetheless had a lot of influence over their husbands and children. Had they always been completely in the background, as some writers have suggested, it seems unlikely that the Athenians could have achieved such greatness in so many areas.

GATHERING CLOUDS

The years from 446 BC to 431 BC had been great ones for Athens. During that period, Pericles had been elected as a *strategos*, or general, every year, and his influence with the Athenian people was at its peak. Athens's powers had hardly been challenged, and there had been only one serious revolt among her allies when the island of Samos, off the south coast of Turkey, took up arms in 440 BC. Pericles himself led the Athenian forces as commander, and after a bitter campaign laid siege to the main city on the island. Nine months later, Samos surrendered. Much more typical of this period was the expedition that Pericles made to the Black Sea to show off Athenian power and to establish Athenian influence with the local princes there. The Black Sea area was important for the Athenians as much of their corn and their wood for building ships came from there.

After 431 BC, the Spartans were becoming increasingly worried about the power and ambitions of the Athenians. During the years of peace, the Spartans had watched with growing resentment as the Athenians secured their hold on the Aegean Sea and its rich commerce while continuing to receive tribute or taxes from all the coastal cities. The city of Corinth had also become envious of Athens's success, and her citizens still wanted to get revenge for the brutal slaughter of her soldiers in 459 BC. Even in Athens itself, there was a certain degree of restlessness. For some ten years now, the navy had seen no important action, and it was unlike the Athenian oarsmen to be happy with that. Pericles himself saw war coming. Aristophanes, the comedy writer, suggested that Pericles was responsible for the outbreak of war. In fact, there were a number of causes. There was a general feeling from 435 BC on that war was not far away.

It started a long way from Athens and Sparta. Corcyra (modern-day Corfu), a state on the northwest coast of Greece that had been founded two hundred years previously by Corinth, came into conflict with her mother city.

Sculptures of two strolling actors wearing comic masks

Fearing that they would be defeated by the stronger forces of Corinth, the people of Corcyra asked Athens for help. Athens might well have refused, but the Athenians did not like the idea of Corinth taking over the navy of Corcyra. At the time, it was the strongest navy in the area after the Athenian and Corinthian navies. The Athenians chose to form a defensive alliance with Corcyra and sent out a small detachment of ships to help. The Corinthians were not amused. They put pressure on Sparta to help and to declare war. At first the Spartans hesitated. The king of Sparta at the time was actually a personal friend of Pericles' and was not keen to get embroiled in a long and costly war. The Spartans stalled for a couple of years. Then Athens treated her neighboring city Megara with considerable arrogance, refusing to allow the Megarians any access to Athenian markets, and Sparta became more willing to consider war. By this time, Athens was also becoming embroiled in a conflict with one of her allies in northwest Greece, Potidaea, and now the idea of war became a real possibility for Sparta and her Peloponnesian allies.

Up until this point in Athenian history, we have had to rely on the writer Plutarch for most of our information. With the approach of the

These ruins are of the Temple of Athena and Hephaestus, built on a hill to the west of the Acropolis.

Peloponnesian War and Pericles' final days, we have a second first-rate source, the historian Thucydides. He provides a brief summary of the fifty years between the Persian wars and the Peloponnesian War and then goes into the causes of the Peloponnesian War in considerable detail. His account includes the debate at Sparta when Corinth and other allies tried to persuade Sparta to declare war. An Athenian was present and spoke arrogantly about Athens's power. The pressure from her allies on Sparta was intense, and war was finally declared.

Did Pericles and the Athenians want a war at this time? Certainly it is hard not to see some of Athens's actions as being provocative and calculated to upset the states in the Peloponnese. Furthermore, Pericles was very clear about how the war should be fought, and Thucydides recounts one of his speeches where he tells the Athenians what they must do, both in preparation for the war and in their conduct of it. While Thucydides does not claim to be repeating the exact words of Pericles in speeches like these, there is no doubt that the style, tone, and content ring true.

Sea power is of enormous importance. Look at it this way. Suppose we were an island, would we not be absolutely secure from attack? As it is we must try to think of ourselves as islanders; we must abandon our land and our houses, and safeguard the sea and the city. We must not join battle on land with the greatly superior forces of the Peloponnesians . . . I could give you many other reasons why you should feel confident in ultimate victory, if only you will make up your minds not to add to the empire while the war is still in progress, and not to go out of your way to involve yourselves in new perils . . . We must realize that the war is being forced upon us, and the more readily we accept the challenge the less eager to attack us will our opponents be. We must realize, too, that, both for cities and for individuals, it is from the greatest dangers that the greatest glory is to be won. When our fathers stood against the Persians they had no such resources as we have now. Indeed, they abandoned even what they had, and then it was by wisdom rather than good fortune, by daring rather than by material power, that they drove back the foreign invasion and made our city what it is today. We must live up to the standard they set. We must resist our enemies in any and every way, and try to leave to those who come after us an Athens that is as great as ever.

A vase painting of a Greek hunter

This passage gives us some idea of Pericles' range as a speaker, appealing to both the minds and the emotions of his listeners. In fact, in the first year of the war, 431 BC, there was little activity. The Spartans moved into Attica in early summer and burned the Athenian crops and olive trees. The Athenians responded by boarding their triremes and making attacks on various points of the Peloponnesian coast. Finally, toward autumn, the Athenians, once they knew that the Spartans had gone home for the winter, moved into the Isthmus of Megara and destroyed the land around the city. There were casualties, but not very many, and at the end of the year Pericles followed the custom of walking down to the Kerameikos, the funeral area, and making a speech praising those who had died in the first year of the war. This speech has come to be seen as an idealized picture of Periclean Athens and a few quotations will give the flavor of it.

Let me say that our system of government does not copy the institutions of our neighbors. It is more a case of our being a model to others, than of our imitating anyone else. Our constitution is called a democracy because power is in the hands not of a minority but of the whole people . . . We are free and tolerant in our private lives; but in public affairs we keep to the law. This is because it commands our deep respect . . . Our city is open to the world . . . Our love of what is beautiful does not lead to extravagance; our love of the things of the mind does not make us soft. We regard wealth as something to be properly used, rather than as something to boast about. As for poverty, no one need be ashamed to admit it: the real shame is not taking practical measures to escape from it. Here each individual is interested not only in his own affairs but in the affairs of the state as well. Even those who are mostly occupied with their own business are extremely well-informed on general politics. This is a peculiarity of ours: We do not say that a man who takes no interest in politics is a man who minds his own business; we say that he has no business here at all . . . Taking everything together then I declare that our city is an education to Greece.

Pericles had considered every possibility in his preparations for the conflict with the

Peloponnesians, but what happened next could have come straight out of a Greek tragedy. An outbreak of plague hit Athens. Thucydides describes it in detail and it is clear that the disease, which was said to have originated in Egypt, was particularly virulent.

> People in perfect health suddenly began to have burning feelings in the head; their eyes became inflamed and red; inside their mouths there was bleeding from the throat and tongue . . . inside the body there was a feeling of burning, so that people could not bear the touch of even the lightest linen clothing but wanted to be completely naked. And indeed most of all would have liked to plunge into cold water.

Thucydides goes on to describe the despair that affected anyone who caught the disease and the way that the crowded conditions in the city contributed to the speed of its advance. Even worse was the ensuing lawlessness and disregard for normal ways of behaving. It was every man for himself, and it is clear that the whole way of life in Athens came close to breaking down. Such was the fear of the disease that the Spartans, terrified of contracting the plague, abandoned their invasion of Attica early in the summer of 430 BC and returned home. One further result was that for the first time in his life, the people of Athens blamed Pericles for their terrible situation. It was he who had persuaded them to retire behind their walls and not to take on the Spartans in open battle. Crowded inside the city in cramped conditions, they were a natural prey to the disease.

Nonetheless, Pericles saw that the war had to go on. Indeed, he may have felt that people would have a better chance of survival away from Athens. He led a naval force to attack various towns on the Peloponnese and returned home in late summer 430 BC. Upon his return, he found that as a result of the Spartan attacks on Attica and the depression caused by the plague, the Athenians had turned against him. He was deposed as strategos and forced to pay a fine. Even so, they still elected him strategos for the year 429 BC.

But early in 429 BC, Pericles himself came down with a serious illness, though it was not the plague that had hit the city the year before. Plutarch describes it as "a kind of dull, lingering fever, which persisted through a number of different symptoms and gradually wasted his bodily strength and undermined his noble

A bronze statue of the god Poseidon, by Calamis of Athens

spirit." As he lay dying, friends and notable Athenians came to visit him. The visitors gathered around his deathbed and, imagining him to be unconscious, talked about his great achievements: his nine victories as an Athenian commander, his virtue, the extent of his power and his famous exploits. Pericles had actually been following what they were saying and suddenly spoke. He was astonished, he said, that they should praise him for his exploits, which owed at least as much to good fortune as to his own efforts, and anyway other generals had done equally well. Yet they said nothing of his greatest and most glorious claim to fame. "I mean by this," he went on, "that no Athenian ever put on mourning because of me."

These last years had not been easy ones for Pericles. His friends had come under attack, his two sons had died of the plague, and he himself had for a time lost the confidence of the Athenian people. One of the last things he did before succumbing to his illness was to ask the Athenian people to pass a bill that would legitimize his son by his lover, Aspasia. The people agreed to this, and the boy was formally registered as an Athenian citizen and later even became an Athenian general.

The death of Pericles marked the end of an era, and even though his policies were continued in Athens's fight against Sparta over the next ten years, his personality and leadership were enormously missed. He had dominated politics in Athens like no other person from 460 BC to 430 BC, and he had masterminded both the consolidation of the Athenian Empire and the final development of democracy in the city. He had done even more than this, however. He had created a climate in Athens that encouraged writers, artists, and craftsmen to flourish as in no other ancient Greek city. For this judgment, we do not have to rely on a biographer like Plutarch or a historian like Thucydides. We have the original texts of the plays, the original sculptures, and the noble ruins of the temples to make our own assessment.

Even so, Thucydides should have the last word, for he had known Pericles and was aware of his greatness. After acknowledging the quality of Pericles' leadership and the greatness of Athens at the time, he continues:

> Pericles, because of his position, his intelligence, and his known integrity, could respect the liberty of the people and at the same time hold it in check. It was he who led them, rather than they who led him, and since he never sought power from any wrong motive, he was under no necessity of flattering them. In fact he was so highly respected that he was able to speak angrily to them and to contradict them. Certainly when he saw that they were going too far in a mood of overconfidence, he would bring back to them a sense of their dangers; and when they were discouraged for no good reason he would restore their confidence. So, in what was nominally a democracy, power was really in the hands of the first citizen.

It is a powerful tribute and a true one.

GLOSSARY

Acropolis Rocky hill in the center of Athens on which the Parthenon is situated.

Aegean Sea Part of the Mediterranean Sea, to the east of Greece, between modern Turkey and Greece.

Areopagus The old aristocratic council of nobles at Athens whose powers were reduced by Pericles in 461 BC.

Assembly The meeting of all male Athenians over the age of eighteen that was held four times a month.

Attica The geographical area surrounding the city of Athens.

comedies Comic plays produced in the outdoor theater at Athens; most of those we have were written by the Athenian playwright Aristophanes.

Council The group of 500 Athenians chosen by lot at village level to prepare business for the Assembly and to put its decisions into operation.

hoplite A heavily armed Greek infantryman who fought in battle. The Spartans were famous as the most effective hoplites.

Isthmus of Corinth The narrow stretch of land connecting mainland Greece to the Peloponnese.

Kerameikos The area just outside the walls of Athens where the dead were buried.

lyre A stringed musical instrument used to accompany singing and poetry.

Mediterranean Sea The large sea that has its entry at Gibraltar in the west and leads into the Black Sea in the east.

Odeion The covered hall built by Pericles next to the theater for concerts and poetry recitations.

ostracism A meeting at which an Athenian citizen could write down on a piece of pottery the name of a politician whom he thought ought to be expelled from the city. The politician whose name was written most often was expelled from Athens for ten years.

paidagogos A domestic slave whose main job was to look after the children in a family.

palaestra An open square area surrounded by a colonnade where Athenian citizens would practice sports and relax after running.

Parthenon The most famous temple in Greece, built by Pericles (in 447 BC) to replace the temple burnt down by the Persians in 480 BC.

pediment The triangular gable areas at the front and back of a temple, made by the slope of the roof, where decorative sculptures were placed.

Peloponnese The peninsula in southern Greece attached to the mainland of Greece by the Isthmus of Corinth.

Piraeus The port of Athens connected to the main city by walls some six miles long.

Pnyx An open area with a speakers' platform near the Acropolis, where the Athenian Assembly met.

Propylaea The monumental gateway on the Acropolis built by Pericles in 437 BC.

Sophists Teachers who went from town to town teaching students a variety of subjects usually aimed at helping citizens to succeed in politics.

strategos A general at Athens. There were ten generals who were also in charge of administration in and around Athens.

theater An open-air auditorium usually hollowed out from a hillside in a horse-shoe shape.

tragedies Plays with serious themes, usually with a hero fighting against the gods or fate. The famous Athenian tragedy writers were Aeschylus, Sophocles, and Euripides.

trireme A Greek warship, manned by 170 free citizens, whose main armament was its ram.

Trojan Wars Wars between the Greeks and Trojans written about by the Greek poet Homer.

FOR MORE INFORMATION

American Classical League
Miami University
Oxford, OH 45056
e-mail: info@aclclassics.org
Web site: http://www.aclclassics.org

The Classical Association
Room 323, Third Floor
Senate House
London WC1E 7HU
England
+41 20-7862-8706
e-mail: Clare.Roberts@sas.ac.uk
Web site: http://www.sas.ac.uk/icls/
   classass

International Plutarch Society
Department of History
Utah State University
0710 Old Main Hill
Logan, UT 84322-0710
Web Site: http://www.usa.edu/history/
   plout.htm

National Junior Classical League
Miami University
Oxford, OH 45056-1694
(513) 529-7741
Web Site: http://www.njcl.org

WEB SITES

Due to the changing nature of Internet links, the Rosen Publishing Group, Inc., has developed an online list of Web sites related to the subject of this book. This site is updated regularly. Please use this link to access the list:

http://www.rosenlinks.com/lag/peri/

FOR FURTHER READING

Amos, H. D., and A. G. P. Lang. *These Were the Greeks*. Chester Springs, PA: Dufour Editions Inc., 1997.

Flaceliere, Robert. *Daily Life in Greece at the Time of Pericles*. Translated by Peter Green. London: Weidenfeld and Nicolson, 1965.

Kitto, H. D. F. *The Greeks*. London: Penguin Books Ltd., 1991.

Krontira, Leda. *A Day in Pericles' Athens*. Athens: Ekdotike Athenon S.A., 1993.

Woodford, Susan. *An Introduction to Greek Art*. London: Duckworth, 1986.

Woodford, Susan. *The Parthenon*. Cambridge, UK: Cambridge University Press, 1981.

BIBLIOGRAPHY

Aristophanes. *The Acharnians.*
Translated by Alan H. Sommerstein.
London: Penguin Books, 1973.

Aristophanes. *The Clouds.* Translated
by Alan H. Sommerstein. London:
Penguin Books, 1973.

Aristophanes. *Lysistrata.* Translated by
Alan H. Sommerstein. London:
Penguin Books, 1973.

Burn, Andrew R. *Pericles and Athens.*
London: The English Universities
Press Ltd, 1966.

Bury, J. B., and R. Meiggs. *A History of
Greece to the Death of Alexander.*
London: The Macmillan Press
Ltd., 1975.

Ehrenberg, Victor. *People of
Aristophanes.* Oxford, UK: Elsevier
Phaidon, 1976.

Jones, A. H. M. *Athenian Democracy.*
Oxford, UK: Blackwell, 1960.

Kagan, Donald. *Pericles of Athens and
the Birth of Democracy.* London:
Guild, 1990.

Meier, Christian. *Athens: A Portrait of the City in Its Golden Age.* London: John Murray, 1998.

Moore, John M. *Aristotle and Xenophon on Democracy and Oligarchy.* London: Chatto and Windus, 1975.

Morrison, J. S., J. F. Coates, and N. B. Rankov. *The Athenian Trireme.* Cambridge, UK: Cambridge University Press, 2000.

Plutarch. *The Rise and Fall of Athens.* Translated by Ian Scott-Kilvert. London: Penguin Books, 1976.

Sophocles. *The Three Theban Plays.* Translated by Robert Fagles. London: Penguin Books, 1984.

Thucydides. *History of the Peloponnesian War.* Translated by Rex Warner. London: Penguin Books Ltd, 1990.

INDEX

ABOUT THE AUTHOR

Hamish Aird is a graduate of Christ Church, Oxford, England, where he read classical languages, history, and philosophy. He is currently the Sub Warden (Deputy Headmaster) at Radley College, Oxfordshire, England, where he teaches Latin and Greek languages and ancient history. He has traveled extensively in the Mediterranean countries and has led groups of teachers on study tours in Greece.

CREDITS

PHOTO CREDITS

Cover, pp. 10–11, 12, 56–57 © AKG London; cover inset, pp. 3, 20, 70–71 © Scala/Art Resource; pp. 9, 46–47, 51, 60–61, 66, 73, 76–77, 80–81 © AKG London/Peter Connolly; pp. 14–15, 22–23, 24, 27, 30, 34–35, 37, 38–39, 43, 45, 68–69, 86, 88–89, 91 © AKG London/Erich Lessing; pp. 33, 64–65, 75 © AKG London/John Hios; p. 96 © Archaeological Museum, Athens/ Dagli Orti/The Art Archive.

EDITOR

Jake Goldberg

DESIGN

Evelyn Horovicz

LAYOUT

Hillary Arnold